DEDICATION

This book is dedicated to those who took on the money-power: the researchers who had their lives ridiculed or ruined, to the few politicians who had their family members or themselves assassinated; to the conscientious insiders who revealed the secrets of that criminal enterprise to which they could no longer bear to be associated.

"History records that the money changers have used every form of abuse, intrigue, deceit and violent means possible to maintain their control over governments by controlling money and its issuance."

James Madison

FOREWORD

The purpose of this concise precis is to introduce young adults to the main themes behind the money they work for. It is expected to be read by those that already feel something is not right but are looking for confirmation of their suspicions.

It is by no means a comprehensive study, as that would introduce volumes of literature, too grand a scale for the target reader audience.

Instead, with the plethora of internet pages dedicated to exposing in greater detail the creation of money out of nothing, this book is hoped to act as a catalyst and spring-board for their own research.

To assist, a bibliography of the texts that were used in the creation of this summary essay is presented at the rear.

With the vast international crime against humanity that is the printing of currency of no intrinsic value in exchange for your life's work, the student, reader, researcher has nothing to lose in these brief 70 pages but their enslavement.

INTRODUCTION

Each country has a monetary authority which prints their currency. As notes become worn and old, they are burned and replaced by freshly printed notes.

This beneficial and superficial role hides a more sinister role – the real purpose.

These nation-based authorities are usually generally referred to as the innocuous term "CENTRAL BANKS"; also often referred to as Reserve Banks or the Lender of Last Resort.

Central Banks in reality are an exchange mechanism. All human effort and endeavor whether it is the farmer in the field sweating as he toils his land, to the scientific endeavor of planning a Mars mission have one thing in common: the reward for their labour and time is the currency printed by their country's Central Bank. Central Banks exchange all human endeavour for a currency that it prints out of thin air.

The inherent value of the currency itself is almost zero – it is the cost of the printed paper and the human effort of printing that paper. The difference between a $1 and $100 note is nothing, although the relative purchasing power but more importantly the psychology behind the numbers is great. The psychology matters because the public think of printed currency as having real value. It does not. Its value depends on the whims of the Central Bank as determined by the Bank of International Settlements.

The relative value of currencies between nations is caused by Imports & Exports. Japan has no energy and buys gas, coal, oil and uranium. In order to import energy, Japan must buy the currency of the exporter to purchase their goods. This pushes the relative value of the exporter country upward relative to Japan's currency. However, when a country buys Japans products, the Japanese currency rises in relative value. In order to ensure Japans products are competitive compared to the cars manufactured by Korea and increasingly China, the Central Bank of Japan prints more currency, making it relatively cheaper (a process called Beggar Thy Neighbour). This printing of additional currency makes the work of the Japanese labour force (its sweaters & thinkers) cheaper – it essentially reduces their effort to nothing. All they receive for their long hours is a currency their Central Bank prints from nothing. It makes them slaves working towards nothing. Japan has been steadily printing its currency since 1991.

Therefore, the worth and value of humanity is both controlled and consumed by Central Banks as they exchange human effort for worthless paper printed from thin air.

How did we get here?

This concise book attempts to explain simply and will act as a record for future young generations so they may understand the exchange mechanism that has reduced them to a controlled and impoverished battery chicken existence.

PART A – THE SHENANIGANS

Fractional Reserve Loans

Fractional Reserves is the amount of real money an institution must keep as a fraction of its lending. Usually the fraction is 10%. Therefore, if an institution has $100 it can lend out $1,000. The 10% of the $1,000 is real wealth that exists usually as physical gold, but the other $900 has been printed out of thin air. However, of great importance is the usury associated with the loan. Interest is paid not only on the $100 but on the entire $1,000. Therefore, the interest accrued on the $900 which is the responsibility of the debtor to re-pay is based on nothing, as it never existed in the first place.

Many believe that when you get a loan from a bank, they take out the cash from a vault held as savings and hand it over to you at interest. That is not the case. Many loans, especially large size and large volume loans like mortgages are provided by Fractional Reserve Banking. The meaning of keeping a fractional reserve is that a fraction of the loan amount is all that is needed to be held in reserve by the loan issuing bank.

Usually, this amounts to 10%. Therefore, a loan of $1,000,000 means the bank only needs to keep $100,000 in the bank itself. However, the interest rate is applied to all of the loan. Not only is the bank getting interest on its $100,000 of real money the recipient of the loan is paying; it is also getting interest on the $900,000 that it is not required to have!

Simple Interest versus Compound Interest

Simple interest means a direct ratio of the principal is owed. Therefore, a $100 loan at 10% interest owes $110 due to the addition of $10.

However, simple interest does not take into account the time the loan is repaid.

The compounding of the interest, applies additional interest to the previous periods interest. Unlike simple interest which is linear, compounding interest is logarithmic. If a sum is loaned at compounding interest over a specified time span, the longer the time to repay, the greater the interest repaid. Compound interest includes the interest on the principal plus interest on the interests over the loan period. The number of compound periods adds the element of time.

Over a period of 30 years a simple interest loan of $100 at 10% would still we $110. Compound interest gives the lender possibility to manipulate the final amount paid by changing the compounding interval. The shorter the interval, from annually to monthly to weekly, the greater the increase in debt over the principal. By manipulating the interest rate, overall length of time for the loan and the compound interval the amount owed increases phenomenally.

The formula for compound interest, including principal sum, is:

$A = P (1 + r/n)^{(nt)}$

Where,

A = the future value

P = the principal

r = the annual interest rate (decimal)

n = the number of times that interest is compounded per unit t

t = the time the money is borrowed

Pay day loans or credit cards are examples of rapidly increasing compounding loans. If $1,000 is obtained and no repayments are made for 10 years, with a typical interest rate of 25% at a weekly compounding interval, the sum owed rises to $12,109.73.

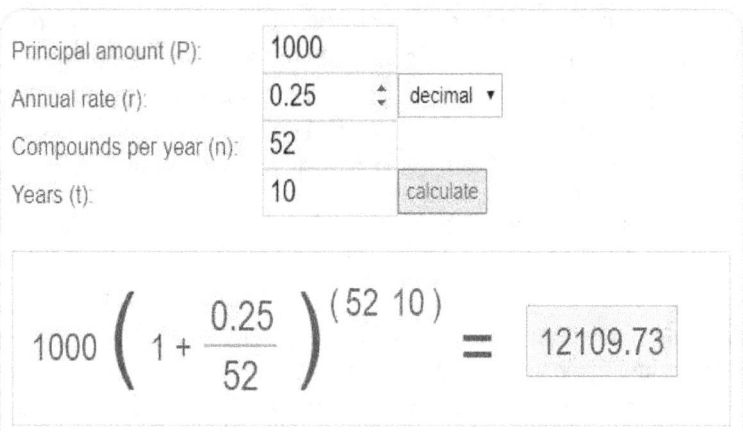

Principal amount (P):	1000	
Annual rate (r):	0.25	decimal ▾
Compounds per year (n):	52	
Years (t):	10	calculate

$$1000 \left(1 + \frac{0.25}{52} \right)^{(52 \; 10)} = \boxed{12109.73}$$

Putting extra currency into an economy lowers interest rates and raises inflation. This is often done deliberately to provide large cheap loans, the interest on which can be raised gradually later, forcing the debtor to work longer and harder. It also causes asset bubbles (real estate, stock market) which can be deliberately collapsed by raising rates, and those in the know (friends of the controlling Central Banks) can be ready to sweep up bargains.

Ledger Duplicity

Central Banks consider a loan to be both a liability (because someone owes you) **and** an asset (because someone owes you, with interest). This double handed perception means any institute that states it has $XX billion in assets could actually mean, it has lent out $XX billion but itself has only 10% of those assets on hand.

Currency versus Money

Gold Standard Currency

Banks gave themselves the power, through corrupt or inept politics, to issue currency notes based on a gold standard to facilitate wealth transfers.

"The Bank of England hath the benefit on interest on all monies which it creates out of nothing".

William Paterson, founder of the Bank of England – the world's first Central Bank, 1693

The original Central Bank, the Bank of England until recently stated that their currency notes guarantee to pay the issuer the value of the note. It doesn't state in gold, but the inference was implied.

Using gold as a measure of wealth with notes backed by gold is fine, unless the wealthy people decide to hoard their gold. If they hoard their gold, there is less available as a tool of exchange. Therefore, a credit system even based on fractional reserve loans is limited. Thereby, limiting Capitalism which means the free exchange of goods.

The amount of gold available on the planet changes. It's an industrial metal. Any gold used on a satellite is lost to finance and commerce as it is removed from the wealth exchange system. If someone loses a gold necklace on the beach, again, wealth is deleted not only from the owner but from any future commerce (should the owner sell the necklace or gift it as inheritance).

Gold is also being found and added to the wealth base of the world by mining. Gold is a marketable commodity like oil. Its value depends on the availability and supply. A rapid addition of gold to a gold-based currency system devalues the basis for the currency.

This occurred when Spanish Conquistadores arrived from South America with gold taken from the Incan Empire. They were instantly wealthy for a while but once their gold had been introduced to the market supply and demand, its value declined.

The Boer War was primarily a banker's war to gain control of the gold and diamonds that had been found in South Africa. The Dutch farmers found themselves invaded, their children murdered in concentration death camps, with their gold and diamond resources controlled by foreign bankers. The British army provided the muscle for the bankers.

If you want to preserve your own wealth, it's necessary to gain hegemony over the world's gold, and then you can control the supply. By controlling the supply, you determine the value.

Capitalism is the free exchange of goods (or services) between mutually willingly participating individuals.

Bankers parasitise capitalism by the currency of exchange (as they produce it) and by changing interest on loans given as a fraction of their real money, should one party in the mutual transaction require cash.

Government parasitizes that transaction with multiple tiered taxes on the same original source of wealth.

The Left dismiss capitalism because of predatory and parasitic banking but it is quite a separate entity. Banking is a parasite on Capitalism.

"Is gold money?"

Ron Paul to Federal Reserve Chairman, Paul Bernanke; a question which he couldn't answer.

July 13, 2011

Petro-Dollar Currency

Many may still believe that a paper currency note is backed by a hoard of gold held at Fort Knox or wherever their government holds their precious metal supply.

In 1971, US President Richard Nixon with advisor Henry Kissinger, and a Salomon Brothers head of the Treasury, acting on behalf of the Federal Reserve central bank, decided to remove the gold backing of US currency. To ensure the currency didn't collapse, Saudi Arabia was asked to always sell oil via OPEC in US dollar currency. Therefore, the currency changed from being backed by free-market gold to free-market oil value. The Saudis got military aid and equipment from the US to protect their oil reserves and they bought US Treasury bonds in US dollars to finance the Vietnam War and the endless wars thereafter.

When banks are involved, your nation's friends become mass-murdering Communists or medieval beheading family-run countries.

However, there is a psychological confidence in the value of the currency in your pocket. Otherwise, supermarkets would change their prices daily depending on the sale value of the oil barrel daily closing price. There is an assumption the world will continue steadily if everyone is confident it will.

Inter-dependent Currency

Free floating currencies (FIAT) became internationally interdependent. If Germans invented a new machine that was in demand, the requirement for their Deutschmark increased to buy those machines. The demand for their currency increased the value of their currency. Germans became relatively wealthier than the countries purchasing their products. Prior to the Euro, Germany devalued their entry rate, ensuring their industrial exports to the Euro Zone which bought 40% of Germany's products.

Similarly, if a large agricultural country like Argentina's agricultural crops fail, the entire population is impacted, as their currency is not wanted by others. They become relatively poorer than other nations and thereby, imports become more expensive for Argentinians.

Is gold money?

After the Bolshevik Revolution, Russia's real physical wealth, its gold, was taken from the Bank of England and given to the USA's Federal Reserve central Bank. In those early days Lenin (real name Ullyianov) may have been the face of Communism (before he went mad) but the real power lay with Litvinov (real name Finkelstein) who put himself in charge of Foreign Exchanges. He repaid the Wall Street bankers that funded the revolution against Russia, by handing over Russia's wealth in gold.

The Bolshevik revolution against Russia was primarily financed by Wall Street Jacob Schiff. He financed Japan in its war against Russia, 1904-05, and funded (and plotted many revolutions such as 1905 using Freemasonry) prior to his success with the Bolsheviks in 1917.

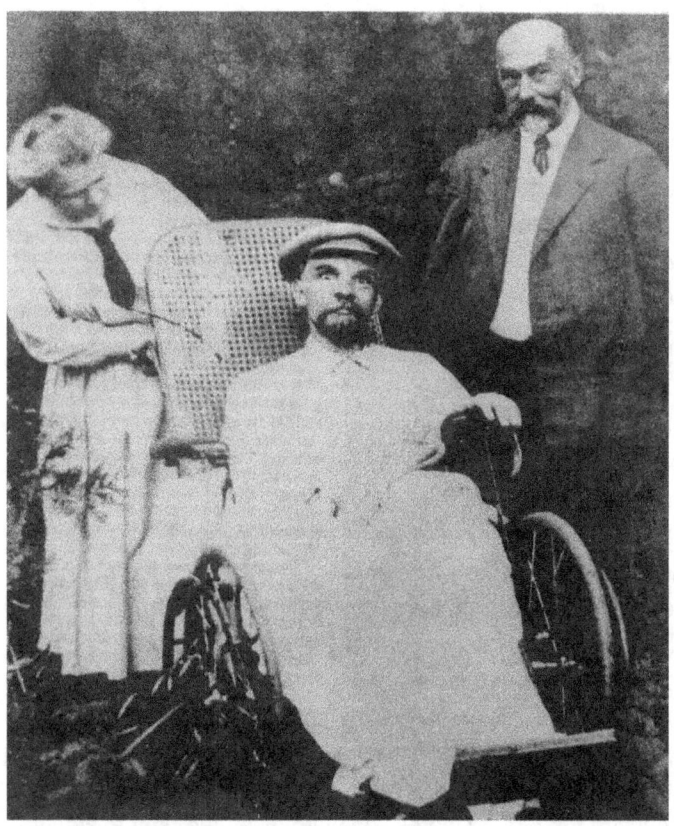

An insane Lenin (Ullyianov) with Wall Street's Jacob Schiff who financed wars and revolutions against Russia culminating in his successful Bolshevik revolution. As a reward, Russia's gold resources were shipped to the Federal Reserve by his revolutionaries.

After the invasion of Libya by Britain and France (both Rothchild cannon fodder source countries), the gold of Libya was held by the Bank of England. Under Gadaffi, Libya was abrogated from the international central banking cabal by its own oil based wealth. Gadaffi had planned a new independent currency for Africa. Britain has fought many wars to ensure its population remains enslaved under the central banking model, the Bank of England. Like a country of Useful Idiot zombies, they have also coerced militarily many other countries into that bondage.

Using its oil wealth to fund a Socialist experiment, Venezuela now destitute, found its gold was being withheld by the Bank of England. It should be noted that Saudi Arabia with a similar level of reserve as Venezuela but using a medieval, theocratic, beheading government, manages its wealth better than Socialism.

In 1933, President FD Roosevelt acting on behalf of the private central bank, the Federal Reserve, issued an Executive Order 6102 preventing the public from saving gold. The publics own gold was confiscated and handed over to the Federal Reserve central bank for a nominal sum. Henry Morganthau (of the infamous Morganthau/Kaufman Plan for Germany) was the Secretary of the Treasury who ordered the prosecution of members of the public that kept their own gold (their money) as conspirators to defraud the USA. The price of gold was later fixed at a higher rate. This allowed more US currency notes to be printed and the reserve fraction in this case was 40%. This funded the New Deal socialist programmes (Clinton Roosevelt – ancestor of FD Roosevelt - had created these socialist plans for the USA) to compensate for the Great Depression. Bankers having caused the Great Depression were given the right to steal the public's gold wealth, make paper notes from it, at 60% more than the gold they had pilfered, at interest via the Treasury which was used to clean-up the mess they made of the economy. Later, Roosevelt used that cash injection as the Lend-Lease Act to provide resources to the

Communist USSR headed by mass-murdering ally and colleague Stalin. The US Presidency seems to have been badly subverted between Wilson and Roosevelt. Roosevelt had many Communist spies in his administration.

South Korea was out of cash during the Asian Currency Crisis of 1998 (induced by George Soros) but unlike the banker confiscation of Roosevelt and Morganthau, the government appealed for donations of gold. The homogenous society of Koreans saw their future and their children's future being compromised and each citizen donated $650 equivalent of their family treasure towards the government coffers to pay off the IMF.

Similar to the US methodology, the Australian Commonwealth can seize the gold of citizens in exchange for paper currency notes from the Australian Reserve Bank.

Gold is money to answer Ron Paul, and currency is worthless paper. That paper can be used to destroy an economy, society, a country either slowly or quickly depending on the rate of Quantitative Easing printing but it inevitably, results in an impoverished public (who have had their work stolen in exchange for the worthless paper).

"Gold is money and everything else is credit."

JP Morgan

Today, only Iran and North Korea remain outside the international currency printing cabal. Recall, "Invade seven countries in five years" by the US General, Wesley Clark.

Keynes versus Reality

John Maynard Keynes was a Freemason Socialist of the Fabian Socialist ilk. Rather than a violent revolution to force the world under the yoke of Socialism (where your property is confiscated and your income tax is 100%), they preferred a soft approach. The soft approach has Useful Idiots to build their own jails while the rest are paralysed by political correctness into inaction.

Central Banks use the Keynesian version of "economics". Again, the joke on the public is that by printing yet more currency, sudden economic busts will be avoided. Rather than a heart attack, which you may survive if prepared, a slow terminal inevitable cancer is used to turn mankind into Socialist slaves.

Keynes ideas are forwarded by Nobel Prize Winners for Economics such as Krugman and Stiglitz who further paralyze the duped masses into complacency and inaction.

The inevitable long march towards economic decline reduces the society to a point where Socialism is inevitable. This was actually Stalin's (real name Dzhugashvilli) method while Kruschev wanted to trickle Socialism into the unsuspecting Western public, bit by bit.

Currency printing erodes the middle class savers, which minimises the upward mobility of the working class. Thereby, demoralizing the entire public into their societal caste.

Keynes as a Fabian Socialist Freemason Banker/Economist joins a league of similar, such as Lord Alfred Milner and Lord Malloch Brown. These represent the Round Table Group, Rhodes Scholars and the Council on Foreign Relations. Their push is Socialism for everyone (loss of property and a slave population) but not for themselves, as they intend to direct the world and its population as "supreme gods on the earth" as elaborated by Klaus Schwab in the World Economic

Forum's insane globalist One World Government plan they call "The Great Reset". Like most socialists, they think they will have an important place in the future, while many are instead simply shot, once no longer useful.

Induced Bank Panics

Banking panics are financial shocks due to sudden worry that deposits may be lost by the public. This leads to an unsuccessful attempt by the public to obtain their deposits from several banks, simultaneously. Banks are unable to restore deposits to their depositors due to fractional reserve loans.

Between 1863-1913, banking panics were further accompanied and complicated by stock market collapse, loan contractions, runs on banks, bank failures and suspension of cash payments to depositors.

One fake excuse for creating a central bank in the USA was to reduce these financial busts and panics. To create an atmosphere to goad the public towards their dream, several deliberately induced panics occurred in the 1800s into the early 1900s. These include:

1819, 1837, 1857, 1860, The Long Depression of 1873-79, 1893, 1890, 1907.

The contraction of credit (elasticity), meaning less loans were obtainable, caused interest rates for existing loans to increase making repayments higher. Many foreclosures or mortgage defaults occurred with small businesses and farmers. Having dutifully repaid their loan for years suddenly their livelihoods were confiscated and sold off. Essentially, they had rented their own farms and businesses until the banks took it off them and sold them.

These artificially induced banking panics are caused and controlled by Paul Warburg's "elasticity". By reducing the available credit, which increases interest rates, or by pumping out too much currency which reduces the interest rates to such a low amount, street bankers cannot survive and they go bust.

Contrary to the repeated claim of ending busts since the creation of the Federal Reserve in 1913, there have been 17 busts with global effects; notably The Agricultural Depression 1920, The Great Depression 1929, the Dot Com Bubble 2000 and the Global Financial Crisis (GFC) 2008 and the government dictated COVID depression of 2020.

After the Federal Reserve Act was passed in 1913, there were four full-scale banking panics, one in 1930, two in 1931, one in 1933 and a localized panic in Chicago in 1932.

Other central banks cause their own local problems such as Black Monday in Britain in 1987. Having pumped up the Yuppie Boom with loose currency printing, the stock market crashed.

"Capital must protect itself in every possible way, both by combination and legislation. Debts must be collected, mortgages foreclosed as rapidly as possible. When, through process of law, the common people lose their homes, they will become more docile and more easily governed through the strong arm of the government applied by a central power of wealth under leading financiers. These truths are well known among our principal men, who are now engaged in forming an imperialism to govern the world. By dividing the voter through the political party system, we can get them to expend their energies in fighting for questions of no importance. It is thus, by discrete action, we can secure for ourselves that which has been so well planned and so successfully accomplished."

Montagu Norman, Governor of The Bank of England, addressing the United States Bankers' Association, NYC 1924. He was the organizer of "informal talks" between central bankers in 1927 which lead to the Great Depression and was again in NYV on April the 7th, 1931 (source New York Times).

Ridiculous Banker Phraseology

Elasticity The driving force behind the USA's Federal Reserve Central Bank, Paul Warburg, insisted that "elasticity" was needed. Elasticity means a currency that can be printed and destroyed at will. The wealth you have in your pocket that you worked and sweated for over several hours per day can be strengthened or weakened by the Central Bank that prints it; if they print more it becomes less valuable (devalued).

Quantitative Easing has been exercised by Japan since 1991 to make its technological exports more attractive (relatively cheaper compared to the currency of the USA and Europe since they use different and separate currencies). During the Obama administration the USA accused the Peoples Republic of China of being a "currency manipulator" as it held its currency at a low rate to ensure citizens of the USA found their products cheaper. However, the USA has been continuously printing since 1913 (confiscated the gold of Russia to print the New Deal) to such an extent that today's dollar is only worth 1% of the original value. The first dollar ever printed is now worth 100 times a present day dollar.

Quantitative Easing is the deliberate programmed excessive printing of currency (out of thin air) by a Central Bank. The overall policy of Central banks is to endlessly print currency until eventually, it truly becomes worthless.

Legal Tender means a currency has a legal status. The Government has backed one currency and any others are counterfeit and not to be used in Capitalist exchanges. The only entity legally enabled to counterfeit the Legal Tender is the central bank, which it does continually.

FIAT is the currency that has been printed by the Central Bank, then given to the Government that makes it Legal tender, but that has no backing to its stated wealth. It may say $100 on the note but in reality, it is no different from the $1 note. It is not backed by any commodity such as gold as in the Gold Standard. Its value depends on how productive, efficient and creative the public workforce because a currency only rises relative to others if the products sold through it are in demand by other countries. If Chinese want Mercedes cars the German currency becomes relatively stronger than the Chinese currency.

Its relative value depends on the efficiency, technology and work ethic of one society relative to another.

Every time a FIAT currency system has been introduced, the authoritative powers, the symbiotic alliance of Shenanigan bankers and government have continued to print the currency to oblivion until it becomes worthless and the country bankrupts. Then the World bank or International Monetary Fund arrive with yet more loans but in exchange for real wealth such as a country's assets – seaports, airports, national airline, mineral resources. Essentially, the country becomes a slave of the foreign internationalist interloping Banksters.

Debt Ceiling refers to the limits of a country's National Debt. Much hand-wringing, anxiety and commotion is made in the media when a country's debt ceiling is reached. The result is always the same. The Debt ceiling is raised and the currency printing continues.

Velocity refers to how fast currency passes through hands. The more hands the same cash flows through, the more times it is taxed. Therefore, the higher the velocity, the more tax extorted and the less real wealth remains.

Price Stability FIAT currencies are not backed by any real wealth. Instead, Central Banks, the issuing authorities of currencies as Legal Tender, state that their banknotes are now primarily for Price Stability. This actually means, they use currency printing to manipulate inflation and interest rates.

CDOs JP Morgan created Collateralised Debt Obligations (CDO) in 1991 at a weekender in Florida. By then, risky investment products were combined with Mum & Dad mortgages to reduce their overall risk level with the investment ratings agencies such as Standard & Poor. Everyone assumed mortgages were stable and were being re-paid, so the overall risk rating category of the products was reduced. However, President Bill Clinton, who was run rings around by bankers made two fatal mistakes. Firstly, he removed the Glass-Stegal Act, which prohibited bankers from casino-style gambling with depositors' savings. Secondly, he stated that every American should be able to buy (*NB: not afford*) a house. This emotionally-driven socialist ideal lead to "sub-prime loans" – loans to those unlikely to have the ability to repay.

Therefore, these mortgage backed products from sub-prime mortgage loans (synthetic-CDOs) were out of control by the year 2000 and JP Morgan got out of them because they realized they had created a monster. When it exploded, these products caused the Global Financial Crisis. The movie The Big Short describes this episode accurately, though omits President Bill Clinton's ineptitude.

Sub-prime loans were suspended and investigated in the USA but bankers being bankers, they recommenced the idea in Australia with many elderly coerced into loans they didn't need or want after a lifetime of fiscal rectitude and many lost their life's work.

PART B – HISTORY

Sumer Time and the Living is Easy

The Sumerians of Mesopotamia employed compounding interest in 2500BC. Scribes for Temple bookkeeping learned how money lent at compounded interest doubled and re-doubled exponentially.

Moneylenders "make a living in their sleep" while others work to repay their loans at an interest rate designed to milk their herd, but not to kill them off entirely.

These loans or debts eventually grow faster than the economy's ability to keep up. This gives the creditor undue claim over the economy. Eventually, their debt claims the sweat and property of the entire society. In societies with a Central Bank, they lay claim over the society courtesy of the taxation system.

Attack at the Abbatoir

About 100BC, Judean moneylenders used to fund Galillean land-owners and farmers. Their hope was not the prosperity of all, the stabilisation of trade and economy, once the loan was repaid. Rather, their deceit lay in subjecting the debtor to a state of perpetual repayment, so that they may do nothing but watch the farmer toil his land, only to give all profits to them.

Galilleans were considered, not surprisingly, rebellious. Into this atmosphere was born Jesus of Nazareth. The spiritually rigorous (such as E Michael Jones and Peter Helland) contend that it was Jesus hours of dying on the cross that changed the direction of mankind's history, after his trial by the Sanhedrin.

However, given the Jerusalem predilection for murdering all Prophets, the areligious could content the moment that sealed the fate of mankind was his attack upon the moneymen of the Temple.

Judeans visited the temple for the Cohen (priests) to sacrifice animals such as lambs which required money. Judeans such as the Pharisees, Sadducees and possibly Essenes were required to visit the Temple during war remembrance festivals such as Purim and Passover, to absolve themselves of their wrong-doing by killing one goat and freeing another (escape goat or scapegoat). This lead to much animal sacrificing and is continued to day during Eid-al-Adha in Islam (which is a sect of Judaism).

Jesus interfered with the moneymen of that animal beheading practice by throwing them out. In Western Civilisation (which adopted the religion he started), he was the first man to take on the bankers and pay their ultimate price.

The scene was depicted in the sketch *"Christ Drives the Usurers out of the Temple" by* Lucas Cranach the Elder, 1521.

The Biblical fight between good and evil for the last 2,000 years goes back to this moment Jesus took on the bankers. Evil is funded through the worship of the god Mammon. Milking the herd is Babylonian while working the herd to death is Judean.

326 years a Slave

Henry VIII, King of England who put himself in charge of the Catholic Church in England, later renamed, the Anglican Church, employed Thomas Cromwell. Thomas Cromwell (ancestor of Oliver Cromwell, the Puritan Republican employee of globalist bankers from Holland) had worked for money-lenders called Frescobaldi (expelled for usury in the wool trade). He lead the example that if Church property (churches, graveyards, monasteries, Benedictine agricultural lands) was confiscated, it could be used to repay moneylenders. That is, Church property could be used as collateral to repay loans, if the monarch (and subjects) became Protestant. This happened elsewhere in Europe, such as Scandinavia. Essentially, a debt ridden monarch could get the bankers off his back by confiscating and handing over Church real estate by converting to Protestantism.

How did monarchs become so indebted to bankers?

Fractional Reserve loans began during the Elizabeth I (daughter of Henry VIII) period. She was run by Khabbalist William Cecil. Henry VIII was influenced by Thomas Cromwell through finances. Around this period usury was banned and reinstated several times. Marrano (not confined by usury) goldsmiths from Spain, accepted deposits of gold for safekeeping. They then offered paper gold receipts for that gold as loans that bore interest. Since nobody was checking how much gold they actually had in safe-keeping, they issued more receipts than the actual real gold they had in their possession. Eventually, that amounted to being ten times the amount of real gold. However, usury interest was/is paid on the receipts, not the actual physical gold. Therefore, interest was paid on the 10% of real gold physical wealth, plus 90% of fake receipt "gold".

The modern extension of these receipts for gold are exchange-traded funds (ETFs) where the receipts themselves are traded but no real gold exists as collateral for the ETF receipts.

Indebted monarchs were culpable for repayment to moneylenders (fractional reserve loans). They garnered wealth from the population by issuing taxation on the aristocracy and nobles. An issue that had given momentum to the Magna Carta. They handed over part revenue of their farms (and conquests). In addition, becoming Protestant, meant Church estates could be seized as compensation to cancel loans.

Prior to the Industrial Revolution, the measure of wealth was land (and gold). A landed aristocrat in Europe may have managed 10,000 acres. To put that into the context of labour, a man using a scythe could cut one acre of hay per day. Therefore, many staff were employed to run large estates. Should his harvest fail, there was no way to pay staff. Enter, the moneylenders. For any loan, collateral was required. The collateral was the land, the estate of the noble.

This set in place a balance of real world value, the many manhours of toil expended on a failed harvest against the fractional reserve loan. Over the years, with successive bad harvests estates were whittled down as collateral for loans, 90% of which were fictitious (just printed paper receipts). Over time, the lenders obtained the estates. They also obtained the noble Lordships that went with the estates procuring positions for themselves in the government, such as the England/Britain's House of Lords. This gave them the power to make laws to suit themselves! Those laws included the authority to wage war, hegemony of the world's resources, using the blood of the public.

Oliver Cromwell was employed by bankers in Holland. His was the original puppet government of the Anglosphere. He was found and installed, by the funders and trainers of his New Model Army, to replace the government (Charles I), install a democracy, purge reactionaries, extract wood (the hydrocarbon of the time) from Ireland to ship build a navy and start an Empire in order to loot the world for those who funded him. Once no longer useful, he was discarded. It took another 50 years for his work to be fulfilled in the time of William of Orange, who continued Cromwell's operation by founding the Bank of England Act.

In 1694, a new model for loans was established. This model became the model for all Central Banking the world over with few exceptions (Iraq, Libya and Iran being examples until invasions replaced the banking model); once operating, it could be offered as a plausible monetary mechanism to fiscally illiterate leaders and the hood-winked masses.

William Paterson, who lost on his Darien Gap adventure - piracy of the Spanish train of silver from Potosi (a 4,500m high mountain of silver) in Bolivia – was the buckaneer used to get the show on the road. On the 21st of June, 1694, a loan of £1,200,000 was given to William of Orange to wage war on France (which was excluded from usury by Papal decree). This was the beginning of banker shenanigans towards the overthrow of Christian Europe – an echo from Jesus' crucifixion.

Opposition to the creation of the bank came from moneylenders that had used the fractional reserve methodology to enrich themselves from nothing. However, this method was incorporated into the bank scheme along with compounding interest. The bank was also given permission to create the equivalent sum in bank notes ie 50% fractional reserve. Later, this was incrementally increased to 10:1, which is the commonly used ratio. Interest due annually was compounded up to £100,000.

The terms of the initial loan on which the initial bank of all banks, the first central bank, the bank of England was established were:

1 that the lenders remain anonymous

2 they be granted charter to open a bank

3 that gold be held as collateral for loans, a metal resource they controlled the supply of

4 that collateral gold reserves be only a 10% fractional reserve of provided loans to either government or individuals

5 that the loan be repaid not by a monarch directly but by establishing taxation on the public

6 usury at compounding interest be accrued to loans

This new model meant the people of a nation were responsible for the governing authority's fiscal profligacy. No longer was a single monarch or his family the debtor, but the entire citizenry and their repayment was coerced by taxation.

"This system of inflation was put into operation by the Bank of England in 1694. The bank was chartered by a company or an association of persons who loaned the English government £1,200,000 and who received for it a perpetual annuity, a right to a series of payments forever from the State. In other words, it created a perpetual debt upon which the people of England must forever pay interest."

Mary Hobart – The Secret of the Rothschilds, 1898

A few years later Scotland was coerced into a union as Britain, joining England's slave population in perpetual debt bondage for a crime they did not commit. In fact, every war, invasion and colonization since 1694 has been to benefit the owners of that bank at the expense of everyone involved: the colonized and invaded had their resources looted and their population rendered servile, the invaders received little other than some trinkets like war medals, mutilation or PTSD.

The bank notes issued by the bank ascribed as legal tender present the statement "Promise to pay bearer the sum of....". This sum has not meant the equivalent in gold since 1931. The promise is not worth the useless paper it is written on. The value of the promised sum is now described as "monetary policy" which is re-phrased as Price Stability. In reality, monetary policy means varying degrees of quantitative easing through three centuries of endless note printing. Price Stability is an unsophisticated phrase for inflation and deflation by currency printing of the banknotes and manipulation of interest rates.

Frankist France – The Grant Orient Experiment

Amshel Mayer Rothchild, a bank employee in Frankfurt, Germany obtained the use of the wealth of Ferdinand II of Hesse-Castel in 1770. Both co-operated on wars and shenanigans, enriching themselves. The relationship changed for their respective offspring. The aristocrat family's wealth was still used, though the profits were kept amongst the sons of AM Rothschild alone. The aristocrats were thus, supplanted. Talmudic marrying of cousins and leasing them out to peripheral aristocrats became a theme. This mixed the bank employees' descendants with the nobility of Europe. As reward for shenanigans and interceding on political divisions, some were given titles such as that of Baron by the Austrian monarch Joseph II in 1783. The power of the Frankfurt shenanigan crime family grew, a black Khabbalist shadow grew over the world. Of the Hidden Hand's 300 members in Frankfurt, it was the Rothschild clan that were chosen to lead the destruction of mankind under banker hegemony funded by the model created as the Bank of England. The Bank of England became the model for central banking throughout the world.

One mechanism to infiltrate and subvert (to *Wallenrod* or create a cancer from within) mankind was the funding of Freemason groups. Grand Orient Lodge was funded by Lionel Rothschild, James Rothschild III funded the Alliance Universal Israel and Karl Rothschild funded the Alta Vendita (Carbonari) of Italy.

The French Revolution, 1789-1798, was the work of the Grand Orient. They killed the nobility, then each other, created the Commune (an early form of Communism) and worshipped Freemasonry's Great Architect (Lucifer). It is possible the writers of the US constitution applied the Second Amendment including Domestic Enemies having witnessed the excesses of the proto-Communist French Revolution. Alliance Israelite Universelle Freemasonry attempted the Revolutions of 1848; thankfully, a failed attempt to create a World Republic (One World Communist Government) across Europe.

Freemasonry arrived from Scotland into France. It grew rapidly and covertly concealed its subversion by outward charitable works and by being considered "god believing". They didn't mention, their actual god is Lucifer. Unfortunately, it was allowed to fester, resulting in the Revolution against France, similar to the Revolutions against England (of Cromwell and William of Orange), the Bolshevik Revolution against Russia in 1917 and the failed Revolution against Spain of 1936. Several minor revolutions and attempts (against Russia in particular) was also Masonic in origin. Freemasonry helped mass-murderer Bela Kun (real name Cohen) get into power in Romania.

Napoleon I was blood thirsty and a suitable candidate for the Rothschild control of France after the Revolution. Like Oliver Cromwell (a member of an early Freemason group headed by England's James I who was initiated in Scotland), Napoleon I had a "mysterious rise" through politics, meaning he was assisted by the Hidden Hand of 300 operating from Frankfurt. Once a revolution succeeded, be it in England or France, that country became a source for promulgating subsequent revolutions elsewhere, though the planning and financing lay with the Hidden Hand first from Frankfurt and later from Switzerland. Those brought up to believe that revolutions are grass-roots and organic movements of the people, may wish to reconsider, and research in detail the events leading up to these "revolutions" and observe who benefitted from the final outcome.

Frankist, meaning Leftist after Jacob Joseph Frank (real name Lejbowicz) France adopted the flag of the revolution. The tricolor stand for "Liberty, Equality and Fraternity in symbolic opposition to autocratic and clericalist royal standards" after nine years of beheading those that did not wish equality forced onto them.

Once Napoleon I was in power, he turned against his hidden handlers and became a patriot of France. Voltaire of the Enlightenment (Illuminated) whose real name was Francis Mary Arouet, never had such conscience other than two deathbed conversions. Napoleon III was an illegitimate bastard from a banker's wife who was rented to an aristocrat to insidiously enter the nobility.

In power, Napoleon I immediately created his own State Bank to abrogate the existing 15 internationalist banks that funded the Revolution against France and buried the country in debt servitude.

"In order for revolution (to be forced onto a nation) first the government must be in huge debt and the public must be paralysed (subverted)."

Captain Archibald Maule Ramsay, MP (of the First Club that opposed WW2)

The Napoleon I bank created on the 18th of January, 1800, belonged to the State and not to the hidden private shareholders like the Bank of England. His bank was based on the agriculture and industry of France and by-passed the moneylenders of the Bank of England. France prospered as the City of London decayed. The French boom included large public works which were funded interest-free.

As Napoleon I controlled the direction of the State Bank himself, the British media following orders from their masters (the example was laid down by William Cecil the Pampleteer) focused their war propaganda directly against him personally. An international cabal of bankers and their puppet governments and Deep State mechanisms in England, Prussia, Austria, Russia and Sweden declared war on Napoleon I because of his bank which had precluded their enslavement shenanigans. Selling Louisiana to the USA bought some funding and time but wars were continuously fomented against France for a decade. By 1814, Napoleon I was finished. His comeback at Waterloo was defeated by the employees of Nathan Rothschild, England and Prussia. Nathan Rothschild used insider information on the battle's outcome to buy Britain through the Stock Exchange.

"When a government is dependent upon bankers for money, they and not the leaders of the government control the situation, since the hand that gives is above the hand that takes... Money has no motherland; financiers are without patriotism and without decency; their sole object is gain."

Napoleon Bonaparte, Emperor of France, 1815

Napoleon I was assassinated for daring to free his people from the yoke of central banking. (A list of those assassinated by bankers is in an Appendix of The Age of Confusion by Seamus bin-Shylockeen).

The banknotes of the bank of France were replaced by the European Central Bank's Euro – a baseless paper note with numbers.

Home of the Slave

Though African slaves were transported to Brazil from merchants in Holland in the 1600s and later the Sugar Plantations of the Caribbean, and north America received Irish slaves (sent by Oliver Cromwell, 1649) then more African slaves, slavery really did not commence on a grand scale in north America until 1913.

President Woodrow Wilson introduced the Federal Reserve Central Bank, the Federal Tax system to feed it by extortion from citizens, got the USA into WW1 and gave Trotsky (real name Leon Bronstein) a US passport and facilitated his journey to Russia. In that year, the Land of the Free became the Home of the Slave.

Several financial panics in the 1800s to early 1900s were deliberately created to scare the public towards a Central Bank system in the USA. Farmers like the Kulaks of Ukraine, lost their livelihoods and homes as interest rates were deliberately lowered, then raised, either making them slaves on their own property or homeless on the street. This inspired the populist movement in the USA which comprised primarily farmers upset with banker legalized robbery.

The US had two experiments with central banking prior to the Federal Reserve Act. As if predicting the Hegelian Dialectic Illusion of Choice (Democracy), both Democrats and Republicans sparred over the creation of the very first Central Bank in the US. Several deliberate banking crises in the late 1800s were used to push the public towards a Central bank – as always, this central bank was to create stability and stop the boom and bust cycle. In her book "Imperialism in America" published in 1893, Mrs Sarah Emery discussed the shenanigans of bankers prior to 1913.

The Aldrich Plan and Federal Reserve Plan (both being the same plan in reality) were proferred as alternatives which would stabilize interest rates, diminish booms and busts. Much as Alan Greenspan, the chairman of the Federal Reserve's in 2007 said, The Great Moderation would end booms and busts.

For a reality check on totally incorrect claim by Greenspan in 2007, just some months prior to the calamitously bad Global Financial Crisis, Congressman Charles Lindburgh in 1913 predicted:

"When the president (Wilson) signs this act, the invisible government from money power, proven to exist by the Money Trust investigation, will be legalized. From now on, depressions will be scientifically created."

Banking and to a lesser degree politics, is the only occupation where inglorious epic failures result in bonuses and career promotions, often onto the UN, IMF or World Bank.

Much like the Bank of England Act in 1694 which was pushed at summer harvest time while the government was absent, the Federal Reserve Act of the USA was introduced two days before Christmas while the government members were either preoccupied or away. Much manipulation was used to trick the public into passivity (paralysis) as the body-count of opponents grew: President Andrew Jackson (attempted assassination), President Garfield (murdered), Louis McFadden (murdered) and Lindburgh's grandson (a German was blamed as fake anti-German war propaganda).

The Federal Reserve's $1 banknote has been the subject of much study by early researchers of the conspiracy against mankind; the pyramid, Novus Ordo (New Order), the all seeing eye, the great seal, the hidden owl, the arrangement of the stars, In God We Trust. Though legal tender, no such promise to pay the bearer exists as on the Bank of England notes. Instead, the Federal Reserve notes have "legal tender for debts, public and private". That innocuous statement underwrites an enormous racket.

In fact, all US$ notes represent debt of the Federal Government. The sleight of hand initiated when Congress requires "money", which is obtained through the Treasury from the Federal Reserve Central Bank is deliberately clandestine. However, it distills to the Federal Reserve creating "money" out of nothing, calling it a debt which attracts compound interest, and results in the production of more banknotes. Therefore, a US$ bank note of legal tender does not represent wealth as the British banknotes pretend, it actually represents debt. That debt is repaid by the workforce in taxes. If the workforce were to pay off all the debt, to repay the national debt of the USA, all notes would disappear, as they are basically IOUs on a magically invented fake debt. If you have US$1 million in your bank account or under your mattress, that means the US tax-payers owe that amount to the Federal Reserve as an interest-bearing debt!

Since the initial $1 banknote printed in 1913, todays $1 banknote is only 1% of the initial real world value; meaning in 2020, the $1 note is worth 1c of a 1913 dollar note. Through the last 107 years, the billions of taxes taken from Americans and misdirected towards their fake national debt has not reduced the debt at all. The debt has instead increased monumentally due to the continuous note printing. Americans have sweated, toiled, manufactured, created, invented their way under a mountain of servitude to a Central Bank.

Can you imagine how wealthy the USA would be, if the population's lives work since 1913 had not been stolen in exchange for worthless paper notes? While Americans work for a dollar, the Central Bank or Counterfeiting Bank or really, the Conspiracy Bank, prints millions per day from nothing. You work for a dollar while they are printing them. If you were in charge of the printing press, you could buy up real assets, before the new injection of currency inflates them.

The USA has $50 trillion of Credit in its economy and only $3 trillion of real Money. The currency that has been printed since 1913, has rarely been extinguished. That is why it is now only 1% of its value.

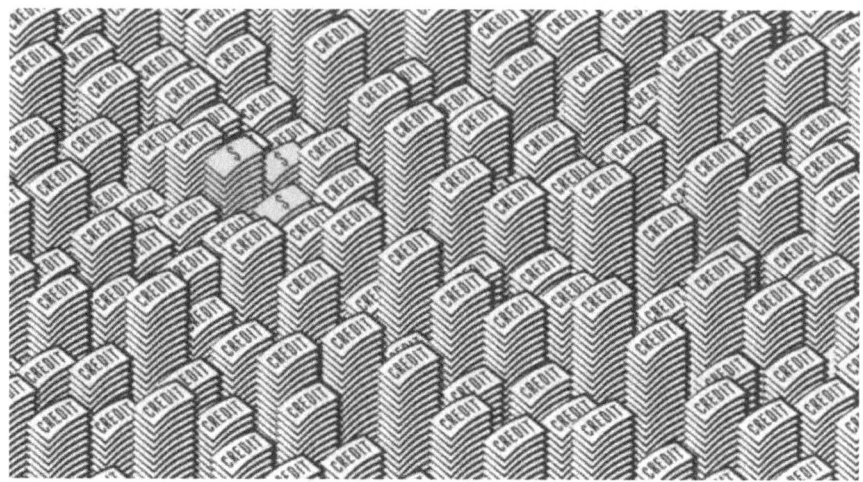

From How the Economic Machine Works by Ray Dalio, 2013. The USA has $50 trillion in fake credit money (currency) and only $3 trillion in real money in its economic system.

On a number of occasions in the last few decades, US Senators have questioned the Federal Reserve board members when something does not appear right. The board members defiantly explain the process to the Senators. Then the investigation disappears. Once Senators realise that it is their own desire for power that initiates the currency printing process, the story and investigation disappears.

Due to freedom of information and free speech legislation (currently under attack) the US banknote currency printing process is the most openly observable. G Edward Griffin's "The Creature from Jekyll Island" book, Mike Maloney's "Hidden Secrets of Money" video series and "The American Dream Film" (just 30 minutes long), explain the process.

In 2009, during the Global Financial Crisis (having a Conspiracy Counterfeiting Central Bank in control of your money means there is a permanent currency crisis) Senator Alan Grayson asked the Federal Reserve's own Inspector General Elizabeth Coleman where US$9 trillion in off-balance sheet transactions had disappeared. At the time, this number represented US$30,000/per American. He concluded: "I am shocked to find out that nobody at the Federal Reserve is keeping track of anything."

Forbes published an article titled, "Is the Federal Reserve using money-laundering techniques to cleanse bank's balance sheets?" on the 29th of October, 2012. It stated, "like (laundering) hedge funds, the Fed is the perfect vehicle to turn bad assets into good. It is weakly overseen (Senators disappearing the investigation) ... secret and anonymous....don't ask because we won't tell....immediately after the 2008 financial meltdown, the Fed laundered US$2 trillion in worthless assets held on the balance sheets of private banks". It continued, that Quantitative Easing is money laundering.

Congress discusses the official Federal debt, but ignores the unofficial off-balance sheet debt. Without the knowledge of Congress, the Federal Reserve secretly gave US$19.6 trillion to Wall Street investment banks. US$11 trillion was given to other Central Banks. The Federal Reserve has been used to bail-out businesses and banks by the US tax-payer since it was introduced (See The Creature from Jekyll Island by G Edward Griffin, 1994).

By 2019, the US Social Security had a US$9 trillion deficit. This unfunded liability (the Federal Reserve is busy saving other private banks through its off-balance laundering facility) means elderly Americans will not receive their promise. It also means younger working Americans could be straddled with $43 trillion in additional taxation but they will get nothing in return, because the national pension system owes $43 trillion more than it has in assets. Enron and Lehman Brothers (previously Kun & Loeb, who were heavily involved in the Bolshevik revolution) had off-balance (hidden) liabilities greater than their assets. The collapse of Lehman brothers initiated the GFC, yet the US national pension scheme is in a far worse condition and it keeps getting worse.

The Inform Act is looking beyond the USA at 40 other countries that are heading the same way. The IMF is eyeing up these countries and its beginning to feel like the Great Reset of the World Economic Forum, where the IMF cancels all debts for ownership of the population.

The owners of the Federal Reserve Central Bank are: Rothschild Bank of London and Berlin, Lazard Brothers of Paris, Israel Moses Sieff Bank of Italy, Warburg Bank of Hamburg and Amsterdam, Shearson American Express, Goldman-Sachs of New York and JP Morgan Chase Bank. JP Morgan were involved with the Bolshevik Revolution against Russia, funded the USSR, prolonged WW1 by 2 years to make good on investments and created Collateralised Debt Obligations, that precipitated the Global Financial Crisis.

Wilson introduced the Federal Reserve privately-owned Central Bank. However, such a currency printing entity is of no use unless a legal framework is instituted to feed it by taxes on the public. Your work is exchanged for the worthless paper it prints via taxation. Therefore, Wilson coincidentally introduced an unconstitutional Federal taxation system which turned American citizens into slaves of the Federal Reserve Conspiracy.

"I have unwittingly ruined my country. A great industrial nation is controlled by its system of credit."

Woodrow Wilson, 1913, after he helped create the Federal Reserve central bank

The Bureau of Internal Revenue was replaced by the IRS in 1953 by the Secretary of the Treasury GM Humphrey. This converted taxation on the US public into a privately owned Trust that was based, not on US soil but in Puerto Rico.

Quite the opposite of Napoleons I's State Bank funding large national infrastructural projects from interest-free money, Roosevelt confiscated the gold of US citizens and used the gold looted from Russia after the Bolshevik Revolution (shipped by Litvinov, real name Finkelstein) to fund his New Deal which was modelled on his grandfather's "The Science of Government based on Natural Law", 1841. The transfer of the wealth of Russia after the Bolsheviks came to power, to the Federal Reserve was facilitated by the Fed Chairman, William Boyce Thompson, who gave $1 million of his own money to promote Bolshevism in Western Europe, particularly Germany.

This cycle of boom, bust, liquidity increase, and liquidity contraction is managed and determined by Central Banks. If you are in the clique of bankers that know the cycle, are informed when changes will occur (e.g. Fed Chair Yellen in 2015), you can't help but become a multi-millionaire through asset purchases before they become inflated.

To finish, slaves do not pay taxes. The liberation of African slaves in Brazil and the US colonies introduced them to the tax system, as slaves bonded to a new master i.e. bankers.

Intoxicating Swindles

Bernie Madoff is a recent infamous swindler who ran a Ponzi investment scam. None of the cash he received for investing was actually invested. Instead he had a floor of old dot matrix printers produce fake statements every month with fictitious gains: just percentages printed on paper, a bit like FIAT currency. None of it was true.

Prior to the GFC, stock markets were booming and free-roaming capital (private equity) was looking for investments around the world. Ireland had weak financial regulation and bankers from Germany used Ireland as a loophole to get around their own oversights. Once the crash occurred the swindlers absconded. The Irish tax-payer was left with massive debts to pay on casino-style banker gambles they didn't even know were occurring and never benefitted from.

Brazil with its national motto of "Order & Progress" is a Freemason experiment. It has a free-wheeling lifestyle, drug culture, low sexual morality, high crime, massive government corruption, nine plane crashes (2016-2018) in two years of politicians that tried to stop corruption – the murderers attended the funerals, a melting pot of multiculturalism, addiction to soap operas, brainwashing TV channels. After the government, Brazil entered a Weimar currency printing phase. Once wages and salaries were paid, the employed immediately bought their weekly or monthly household shopping as inflation was running so high, it would be more if they waited a week. There was a run on banks and overnight the TV announced that all banks are closed and only token amounts of cash could be obtained from deposited savings.

Individual Ponzi scammers once caught go to jail. However, all of Europe's big banks have been fined for money laundering. These are: HSCB, Barclays, BNP Paribas, Credit Agricole Group, Societe General, Deutsche bank, Santander and ING. Australia's Commonwealth Bank was also fined while the CEO attended the Australian of the Year Award! These fines do nothing but repay the tax-payer a little while the shenanigans continues and no banker ever goes to jail. Of all the large corporations fined and fined with regularity, half the number are banks.

Goldman-Sachs assisted Greece to get into the Euro Zone by cooking the books. This caused the Euro Crisis, put Greece through austerity measures which may last until 2060!

During Germany's Weimar Republic several high profile swindlers reduced the life savings of Germans struggling through the Federal Reserve's Great Depression. The currency printing was at such an outrageous level, wheel-barrows for cash were needed. Germany used the financial ideas of Gottfried Feder to get itself out of the Great Depression. Like Napoleon I, suddenly Germany found itself in WW2.

The Financial Services Sector

The Financial Services Sector projects an image of austere stability, intellectual cognisance and professional ability. In reality, the Financial Services Sector does nothing for the economy of a country. It derived merely to put a finger in the wall of the dam created by the Central Banks endless currency printing. Its purpose and the multiplicity of investment products have been created only because the Central Bank is continually devaluing the wealth in your pocket. Therefore, the sector, although pretending to invest and create wealth is merely a façade to lessen the impact of continuous devaluation of your wealth by the Central Bank and Government in their symbiotic conspiracy against you, the taxed.

Constantly devaluing the currency by injecting more and the low interest rates for deposits means savers are forced into investing their savings. This is often with the institutions that created the Libor scandal, scraped pension funds, forex scandals and market manipulations.

HSBC – The Opiate of the Masses

Equating a large bank with drugs and Marxism is not as outrageous as it seems. The Sassoon Family from Baghdad ran the opium dealing business in Hong Kong. The proceeds were banked with HSBC. Britain provided the muscle in the form of the British army. Other notable legalized drug dealers include Kapoor of India and Sackler of the USA.

Britain is blamed for the Opium trade (and wars) by the People's Republic of China but their own dear leader, Chairman Mao, was run by the same Talmudic gang that ran the opium into China.

The association of globalist bankers using socialism to further their goals has been explored by others:

"The drive of the Rockefellers and their allies is to create a one-world government combining super-capitalism and Communism under the same tent, all under their control. ... Do I mean conspiracy? Yes I do. I am convinced there is such a plot, international in scope, generations old in planning, and incredibly evil in intent."

Larry P. McDonald, U.S. Congressman, 1976 in The Rockefeller File, by Gary Allen (1975)

And, explored particularly by Anthony Sutton and Eustace Mullins.

Opium was the only commodity that saved the British balance of payments with Asia from ruinous deficit. Opium merchants instructed Britain that a "just war should be fought to defend progress". In reality, the British leaders of the opium trade through the 1830s and 1840s were far more interested in protecting their drug sales in order to fund lucrative retirement packages (eg James Matheson, used his profits to buy a seat in Parliament and the island of Lewis, Scotland).

HSBC continues to be a banker of choice for drug dealers, such as Mexican cartels.

Bank Fines

Goldman-Sachs were issued a fine for laundering Malaysia's pension fund and JP Morgan were fined for manipulating the price of gold and silver (they're using ETFs to keep the price down while buying up real physical metal).

Really what do these fines mean?

They are merely a temporary minor inversion of the power structure between Bank and Government. Governments work for those banks. They own the Federal Reserve and the government obtains taxes and hands it over to them for the fake debt they print. When a government fines those banks, it is merely reversing the flow of money for a brief period. Eventually, it goes back towards the bank. Banking socializes the world to redistribute its wealth back to them in exchange for worthless currency they print.

Vultures or Milkers

Youth are informed the world's economic ills are due to Capitalism. However, Capitalism (the mutual exchange of goods) is liberating. The People's Republic of China pulled 300 million out of poverty through the Capitalism introduced by Deng Xiao Ping in just 20 years. At the same time, oil bloated Venezuela drove its population into poverty by going the opposite direction having adopted Socialism. A monarchy such as Saudi or Dubai manages an economy more equitably than socialism.

Capitalism is not the problem; that is a Big Lie. What drives once prosperous liberated Western nations towards poverty is taxation and FIAT currency. Both work in unison as the Marxist progressive tax tier removes the incentive to earn more. What you earn from real work is exchanged for worthless FIAT currency bank notes, which can be printed at will. In addition, the more Americans work, the more they drive towards poverty (a less direct method than Venezuela) as the increase in their "money" actually represents an increase in their national debt. The USA is heading towards poverty in a similar route to Argentina.

Paul Singer who sets USA foreign policy along with Bernard Marcus and Sheldon Adelson, owns Argentina as his personal slave colony. Argentina is working its way into poverty. The sweat of Argentines is collected by Singer.

Singer started by buying off ill asbestos workers cheaply, increasing the viability of factories he bought. Then in Peru, Singer grabbed control of the entire financial system and assisted President Alberto Fujimori to escape in return for ordering Peru's treasury to pay him $58 million. Singer paid about $10 million for some "debt" supposedly incurred by the Republic of Congo. To collect on his $10 million, Singer had begun seizing about $400 million of national assets.

Singer sued to get billions, from the government of Argentina for old debt that President Ronald Reagan had already settled. He demanded that a US court, order Argentina to pay him ten times the amount above the Reagan deal. President Obama demanded a USA federal court stop Singer from attacking Argentina. Singer was trying to turn Argentina into his own personal slave colony. Why debt enslave one person through personal loans or a mortgage, when you can mortgage an entire country, with their tax system providing you the fruits of their work? This Vulture has undermined the safety of the entire world financial system by destabilizing every financial rescue mission from South America to Greece and to the Congo.

Vulture funds don't exist to make money on investments. Their method is to make huge profits through extortion and interfering with bankrupt nations as they try to negotiate good terms on debts they cannot pay. Vultures prey on the debts of embattled nations. They "buy the debt" of countries. Similar to the Collateralised Debt Obligations of JP Morgan, though on a bigger scale. It seems the worst investment you could make to a normal sane individual: to buy a bad debt from another. However, the psychopathic nature of these globalist banker vultures like the Judeans did to the Gallileans, have no conscience about forcing a nation's population into permanent slavery; working the herd to death. Buying a nations debt, is the contemporary Slave Market, where the government act as enforcer for the Slave Master through taxation.

The currency printing to cause a fake debt, which is repaid by real effort through taxation, that comprises the FIAT system, is a slow milking process: keeping the herd alive to serve you. The Marxist progressive tax tiered system milks the public differently: the more you earn, the more you work (perhaps in overtime), the more you invest or the more successful you are overall in life, the more you are milked. This creates a disincentive for the working class to better themselves. FIAT currency operations particularly attack the middle class because they earn a little more than needed for basic survival and save their earnings. These saving are eaten away by the termite mandarins of Central Banks. Even when you've worked, paid taxes and saved for a rest, the termites are nibbling away as the Financial Services Sector frantically attempts to stem the corrosion.

PART C- CONTEMPORARY COUNTERFEITING CONSPIRING MODELS

Central banks hold individuals, societies and entire countries to ransom by lowering interest rates, then increasing them to confiscate assets. They create asset bubbles that destroy sections of the community when they burst. They reduce the value of your life's work by continuously devaluing the currency you are paid with.

"The modern banking system manufactures money out of nothing. The process is perhaps the most astounding piece of sleight of hand that was ever invented. Banking was conceived in iniquity and born in sin. Bankers own the earth. Take it away from them, but leave them the power to create money and control credit, and with the flick of a pen, they will create enough money to buy it back again. Take this great power away from the bankers and all the great fortunes like mine will disappear, and they ought to disappear, for this would be a better and happier world to live in. But if you want to continue the slaves of bankers and pay the cost of your own slavery, let them continue to create money and to control credit."

Sir Josiah Stamp, Director and President of the Bank of England during the 1920's

Reserve Bank of New Zealand

New Zealand's (NZ) Reserve Bank uses the same sleight of hand as perfected by the Federal Reserve. One difference, although minor, is the Reserve Bank of NZ's employees are paid from taxes. Therefore, the public are duped into believing it is a nationally owned bank. It was first established in 1934, although it is not a government department but since 1936 had been wholly owned by the government. That is deliberately confusing. It is a colony of imperial international bankers based in Switzerland – as the title of this book surmises, "shenanigans".

The NZ government sell government bonds. These are only available for purchase to a limited few entities. These entities know the NZ Reserve Bank will eventually purchase them. However, the Reserve Bank purchases them at a higher than market value price. This keeps the bond value artificially high which keeps yield low and nationally, the usury interest rate low. The Reserve Bank buys the bonds with new additional currency that is printed and thereby, flushed into the country.

Should the NZ government wish to ingratiate themselves with the public through a new "free" venture, rather than tax the public directly, they issue bonds and the taxation is delayed, concealed and dumped onto future generations.

The national debt of New Zealand (NZ) is relatively low compared to many other English-speaking and developed countries. However, the present Prime Minister (from a female-only Freemason outfit called Job's Daughters) is working hard to undermine their financial independence (and therefore societal independence).

"The banks do create money. You will find it in all sorts of documents, financial textbooks, etc."

H W White, Chairman of the Associated Banks of New Zealand, to the New Zealand Monetary Commission, 1955.

Reserve Bank of Australia

Prime Ministers have often repeated during fiscal instability, that they do not direct the affairs of the Reserve Bank of Australia. Of course, they do not. It is controlled by the Bank of International Settlements in

Switzerland and therefore not an Australian government institution. Like NZ, the Australian tax payer merely funds its machinations against their own interests.

The mechanism in Australia differs from the US model in that the Australian public really are asleep (paralysed). Using the same government bond purchasing trickery out of public scrutiny but superimposed upon that is a direct link between taxation and the Reserve Bank. Australians pay taxes directly to the foreign controlled Reserve Bank. The tax office has its bank account with the Reserve Bank, details below:

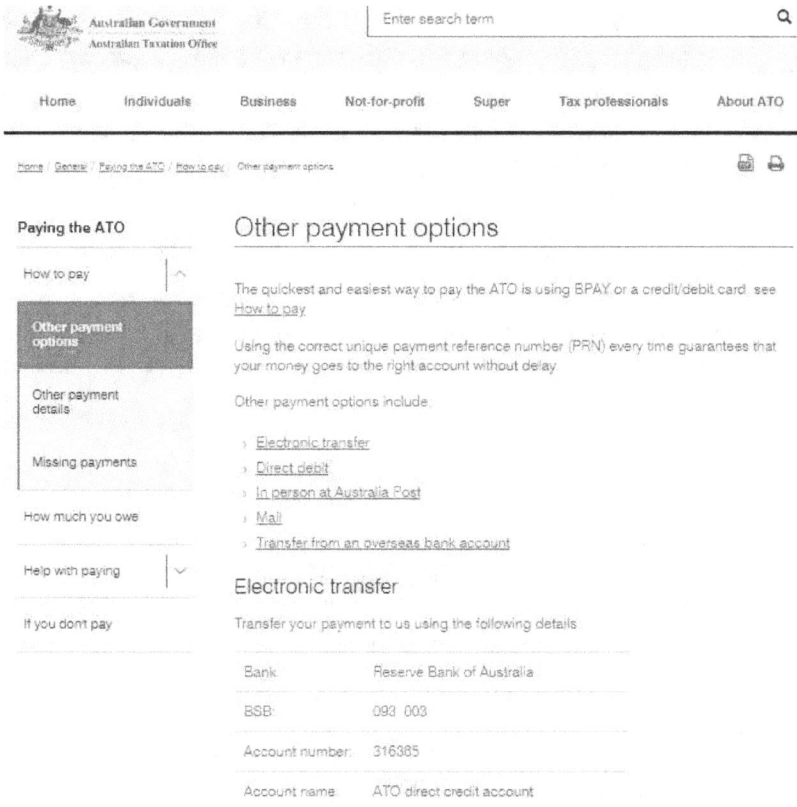

It can be accurately perceived that the Australian government actually works for the Reserve Bank. The Treasury is the go-between that writes the cheques on your children's futures. The muscle to extort the public of their real work, much like the British army was used in Hong Kong and against the Boers, is the Australian tax office.

The same tripartite cabal that milk the American public, operate similarly in Australia. The Treasury, the Central Bank and the Tax Office co-operate to milk the public in plain view.

From the website of the Australian Tax Office, from which many Australians live in fear as do Americans, the bank account for payments is the Reserve Bank. The taxes Australians pay do not go to their government. Instead they go directly to the Reserve bank. The Reserve Bank then gives currency to the Australian government for welfare, roads, hospitals and schools.

If you imagine, you give the Reserve Bank A$1,000 in tax of real money you sweated to generate. As a fractional reserve ratio of 10:1, your real work can be used to print A$9,000 of fake currency. The government gets a new sum of A$10,000 and a fake debt is created for A$9,000.

Australia runs a national pension scheme paid directly from employers and workers not from taxation called Superannuation. The government forces the public to hand over their earnings but does not guarantee there will be anything there when they retire. About 80% of Australians die before reaching the age required for their Superannuation (their own money) can be accessed. This is in direct opposition to how Singapore runs their Central Provident Fund. It is guaranteed by the government. What you put in, you will get out at a minimum as index linked to inflation. Pensions are often heavily invested in the Stock Market. Generally, the Stock Market rises (aside from the regular planned central banking induced busts and recessions) over time. However, the currency used to liquidate assets from sold shares, always go down. Currency printing is sometimes described as an unseen stealth tax.

Scandinavia

Norway, Sweden & Finland, once unified as Scandinavia, sold itself to globalist bankers when the monarch, Gustav I Vasa, converted to

Protestantism, confiscated Church property and gave it to moneylenders.

Norway, Sweden and Finland's Central Banks continue the same vague, jaded and totally untrue claims about being there to promote "price stability". Norway's Central Bank (Norges Bank) has a webpage praising itself called "Why are banks so important?" This advertising brochure completely omits fractional reserve loans, dubious government bond shenanigans inventing debt, currency printing and taxation on the public herd to repay the faked debt. Sweden's Sveriges Riksbank continues the same "monetary policy", financial stability", "inflation target" but nothing about working your way into poverty because of their racketeering

European Central Bank

The Euro notes move even farther from the Bank of England and Federal Reserve banknotes. They bear no promise to pay, nor religious belief and are merely coloured paper with numbers on them. They are purely FIAT more similar to the People's Republic of China's yuan notes. China was the original creator FIAT notes in the 11th century.

Communist China seems the model for a One World Government. It was Stalin's idea to create large trading blocs such as the EU to increment its implementation. Trotsky wanted an immediate bloody revolution to continue the socialist world revolution's of 1848 but Stalin preferred subversion and the long march to create a happily enslaved compliant population over endless killing. Debasing Western "hard-currencies" into Communist paper is one route to that goal.

Less than 10 years after the introduction of the Euro FIAT currency, the ECB was busily printing it in crazy amounts. Ridiculous, child-like and inarticulate globalist terms like "bazooka" and "helicopter" were introduced. The idea was that printing a helicopter's worth of currency and throwing it around like confetti would solve economic problems. This is a child's dream, yet these imbeciles are the ones in charge of our lives, our children's hopes and our grandchildren's futures.

Mario Draghi, a Maoist Communist, who donned a suit instead of an Orwellian party uniform, initiated the ruinous scam. The often inebriated Jean-Claude Junkers of quotes that include: "Sometimes you have to lie. We don't tell the public what we are doing but do it anyway. I'm for deep dark debates," created the ridiculous term "bazooka" to describe how worthless Euro banknotes were to be fired at the EU Zone to "save the Euro". What is the purpose of the new banknote that it needs to be "saved"? By now, you should know.

For 10 years the ECB printed useless banknotes. It ceased in 2018, then started up again within two years for the COVID government induced recession.

Bank of Canada

At this stage of this precis, Canada's Central Bank provides some needed humour. Their motto is: " We are Canada's central bank. We work to preserve the value of money by keeping inflation low and stable."

The result of their work is the complete opposite: over time, the value of the currency is destroyed as it is continuously printed.

Bank of International Settlements

The Bank of International Settlements (BIS) was founded in 1930 but individual shareholders were bought out in 2001. However, much as the Bank of England was nationalised in the 1970s, it doesn't matter much in the end because the owners would not relinquish real control, but continue from the shadows.

The original shareholders were replaced by the world's central banks as the new owners. *Yet it buys "tradeable securities" from central banks.* Therefore, it is a laundromat, on a global scale, that dwarfs the Federal Reserve's laundering.

The BIS is the controlling authority of the world's separate central banks. You work for your government through tax extortion. Your government works for the local central bank. Your local central bank, works for the BIS. That is the banking hierarchy of globalism.

The BIS is pushing for an entirely digital currency rather than printed paper. This would lead to every individual person's spending habits being open to scrutiny and ultimately spied upon by their local main street banks, through the central bank onto the BIS with their government's cooperation. The government's role is to ensure that taxes keep flowing upward to service printed fake "debt." Governments work for central banks.

Norway and Sweden currently spy on citizens' bank accounts. If a relatively large sum of cash (per your income) is taken from or entered into your bank account, the government like in a futuristic dystopian horror movie, is aware. It would lead to the public being branded like farmed cattle and confirm ownership of your work and activity by the banking hierarchy.

The Cabal

If the GFC of 2008 (and ongoing) taught anything, it is that banks order governments around. The US government was threatened by the banks on Wall Street that they would collapse the USA, the world's biggest economy, unless they were given a bail-out using tax-payers money. This is not unusual. In fact, every Central Bank Act states that the tax-payer is responsible for debts (real or faked).

Central Banks protect the casino-style gambling debts incurred by investment banks and commercial banks (the vehicle used for flooding the economy with freshly created currency) by ordering governments to bail them out.

This was summed up by this phrase popularized after the GFC: "Privatise the profit. Socialise the debt".

The power hierarchy between the international cabal of banks (controlled by the BIS) and subservience of the world's governments is thus revealed. Obedient government usefulness to the cabal, is their continued increase of fake debt and their extortion of the public for taxes to service (not re-pay) "debt" while providing the occasional school, road and hospital, like trinkets to ensure the public's loyalty. Welfare is used to enforce loyalty.

Welfare is used by governments to create a lower caste of dependent Welfare Clients. Welfare recipients are actually termed "clients" in some countries. They are obedient clients of the State. Currency hand-outs are used as the carrot to control their obedience and if that fails, the State has the right for coercive control measures which can be used as a stick.

"The invisible Money Power is working to control and enslave mankind. It financed Communism, Fascism, Marxism, Zionism and

Socialism. All of these are directed to making the United States a member of World Government."

American Mercury Magazine, December 1957, page 92

The BIS has had three meetings Basel I, Basel II and Basel III. *"The BIS are forcing their home governments to get in line, as has the UK, the US and most other developed nations. It is truly a global rule by central bankers acting in concert/cabal. The proposed Basel III regulatory capital requirements are an immense and unnecessary burden ... new regulations will further drive consolidation into a few bigger banks... further consolidating wealth in fewer and fewer hands. That is the object – world bank/economic and hence political control by a handful of un-elected, unaccountable, international bankers beholden to no one, many of whom have ethics only Machiavelli could admire and worldviews that most people on earth would consider abhorrent."*

Patrick S.J. Carmack, 2020 of The Money Masters

PART D – CONSPIRACY EMPIRICISM

National Debt

Governments in more socialised countries are elected on promises of gifts to the public. Increased public services are attractive in modern Western democracies, where the traditional husband role has been replaced by government. Feminism has replaced the male provider-protector role with government. The etymology of the word "husband" means economist.

What the government is not saying, is that the cash used for their promises comes from the public via taxation. If the government cannot garner enough funds to pay for their promises from taxation, they borrow.

"The few who understand the system will either be so interested in its profits or be so dependent upon its favours that there will be no opposition from that class, while on the other hand, the great body of people, mentally incapable of comprehending the tremendous advantage that capital derives from the system, will bear its burdens without complaint, and perhaps without even suspecting that the system is inimical to their interests."

The Rothschild Brothers of London & Berlin writing to associates in New York, 1863.

As single households increase in number and especially single parent households, the burden for tax production falls increasingly onto the male population, whether single or married.

Males predominate in wealth producing roles. For a country to increase in wealth, in this technological world, inventiveness keeps you ahead. This provides your intellectual base with export markets for their creativity and productivity. Women predominate in employment roles where the wealth source is derived from redistribution – either from company to company in services or from taxation in government roles.

Whether your export is food or raw materials, technological input increases the productivity, increasing your profits.

"It is well that people of the nation do not understand our banking and money system for if they did, I believe there would be a revolution before tomorrow morning."

"The one aim of these financiers is world control by the creation of inextinguishable debts."

Henry Ford, Ford Motor Company, 1936

In order to pay for a country's borrowings, inventive schemes of taxation are needed. Tax upon tax upon tax are necessary and stealth taxes are invented. Company tax is 30%, and then a company has 70% left to pay its employees, pay for machinery, fixtures, fittings, and Research and Development. The employees pay income tax on their share of the remaining 70%. If the employee requires a plumber or electrician at home, they pay from a wealth source that has already been taxed twice, then those tradesmen pay tax from their income. The same wealth source is taxed 3 times, minimum. In addition, all items purchased have a GST/VAT tax. All of this tax upon tax from the wealth source is increasingly used to mainly service the governments' borrowings: its national debt; a faked "debt."

The Debt Pyramid

Imagine if a lender has $1,000 to loan. He gives $100 each to ten people. They in turn each give $10 to another ten people. The initial lender demands 10% interest for his $100 from each of his ten liable persons. They in turn charge 10% interest on their $10 loans.

If the initial $1,000 has been borrowed (at usury interest which is compounding), the quicker this debt is repaid, the less compounded interest has accrued. To pay if off quickly, the lender needs to chase those 10 guys that owe $100, at interest. They in turn each need to chase the 10 guys that owe them $10, at interest.

This creates an ant colony lifestyle, where all levels of society scramble to send their work upward before their debts increase. In order to ensure the interest does not accrue on their loans, the one hundred people at the bottom of the pyramid must scramble through life paying the interest and principal upward. The pyramid's mid-level lenders must also scramble through life as they owe the initial lender at the top.

The compounded usury interest on this hierarchy of debt, trickles upward in floods to the top; the 1% are bankers.

Tax upon Tax upon Tax

A Corporation uses its generated Wealth to pay corporate tax to their local government. Usually this is about 30%. This leaves 70% of their earnings. Of that 70% , perhaps half, 35%, goes to employees as wages. Employees pay income tax on their wages. Following Marxian policy most governments charge a Progressive Tax Rate – the more you earn, the more of your work taken as taxation. On top of that the employee pays many other taxes such as property taxation, taxation of the power and water consumption, tax on transport and tax on the fuel to commute.

Therefore, as each employee begins each day, they have already been hit with several taxes, i.e. their work has been severely punished before entering the work place. If they are late for work they may speed and be hit with a speeding fine (another term for tax). These are taxes upon the Cost of Living before a penny is earned.

Perhaps, the Corporation's employee spends a month's salary on some home renovations. A contracted tradesman pays a second income tax on the same initial wealth source. In addition to the income taxes depicted in the table below, there are a plethora of other peripheral taxes involved in any human endeavor or transaction (Capitalism).

Corporation	Capital	Tax
Earnings	100	30
Wages	70	
Employee	40	30
Renovations	30	10
Result	**30**	**70**

The government tax office is the net beneficiary of the human endeavor from the initial Corporations wealth creation, from a minimum of three tiers of income tax (plus several other taxes)

This sub-contractor also pays a Marxian Progressive Tax and the plethora of other taxes involved in just daily living. The Corporation's employees are encouraged to be efficient by sub-contracting skills they either do not possess or do not have time to acquire. This means more sub-contractors are needed just for daily living in an urban environment. More sub-contractors means more Taxation on the same Corporation's Wealth.

Every time currency leaves your pocket and goes to government it is a Tax regardless of the clandestine phrases (levy, rates, fees, fines) used to conceal what is actually occurring.

Governments tax behavior they wish to reduce such as smoking cigarettes. Given the Progressive Taxation of Marx and the huge numbers of taxes the employed shoulder each day, perhaps Western developed governments do not want the public to succeed in life; a demoralszed, paralysed, taxed plebian herd is easier to milk – just slightly more independent than Welfare Clients.

The Tax Pyramiding

Tax Pyramiding is the phrase used to describe the tax upon tax upon tax of raw materials, through production onto consumption of the final product. A pyramid shape can be used to describe some events in banking but this sequential taxation is not accurately described as a pyramid.

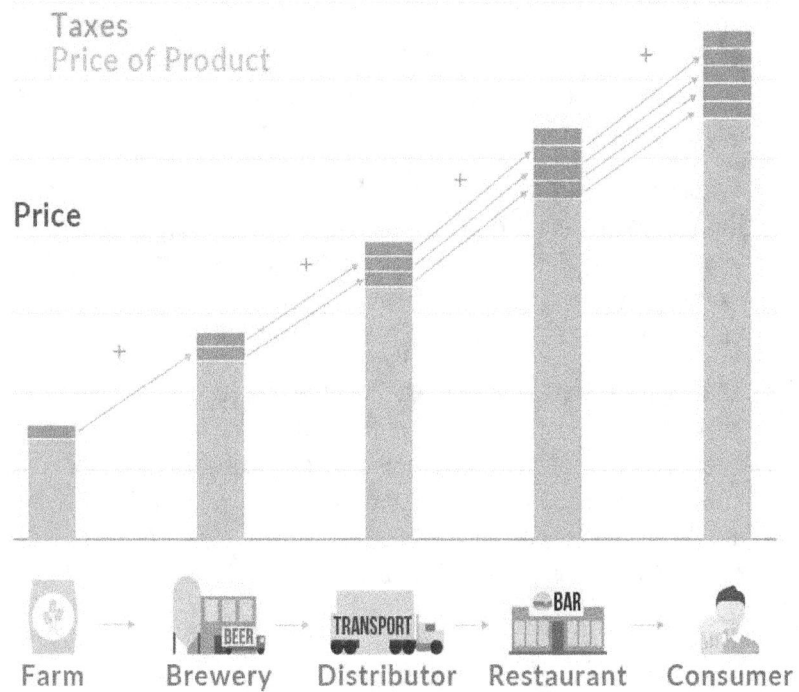

Price

Taxes
Price of Product

Farm   Brewery   Distributor   Restaurant   Consumer

Stages of Production

Every human endeavour attracts taxation from the water you drink to the food you consume. The only item not taxed is the air you breathe, although that last remaining free avenue has been captured by a tax on CO_2.

Continuous Growth

For a continuously growing national debt, welfare system, an aging population's medical needs, dilapidated infrastructure, countries need continuous growth.

Increasingly, tax burdened and Cultural Marxist conditioned Europeans are opting out of the traditional nuclear family. Women are informed that this model is oppressive by feminism. Males increasingly can't afford a family because accommodation is expensive due to Quantitative Easing's asset bubbles.

This population stagnation causes the tax upon tax scam the government is running to pay off their promises to be under-funded. Therefore, they push for mass-immigration in the assumption that the newcomers will be automatic new tax units to harvest. Increasingly, the opposite is happening and the immigrants are a growing burden on the increasingly diminishing tax base.

"The American Republic will endure until the day Congress discovers it can bribe the public with the public's money."

Alexis de Tocqueville 1835

A sole male, realises he needs far less money to live on by himself than if he is providing for a family. Soon, he realises the more work he is doing, the more he is being used as a husband for mass-immigration, multiculturalism and the female workforce. Eventually, he realises, they can do a lot less work than his father to survive alone.

The model of government promises funded by borrowings to an increasingly dwindling population and smaller families, needs continuous growth. The solution to the Cultural Marxist and Feminist attack on society is mass-immigration, which is yet more Cultural

Marxism. Today, European youth are brainwashed to not have families or children in order to save the environment.

Mass-Immigration Ponzi

A Ponzi Scam is a hollow investment, where constant cash injections are needed to give back to those opting out. No actual investing or wealth is being produced. The manager of the scam is living, often lavishly, from the cash being injected, while the ones opting out must get more than they paid in, otherwise the scam would be a poorly performing investment.

The national debt compounding at usury interest must be fed. As the taxation base dwindles by decreasing male productivity (as there is no need to over-work to have the effort taxed and given away) developed countries require continuous population growth to provide a taxation base and a consumer base to keep feeding national debt.

Australia runs a Superannuation pension scheme which is an example of a Ponzi Scam that has not collapsed yet. A portion of a worker's salary is taken and invested. The public are warned to not invest in the stock market with money you can't afford to lose, but in this scam, the government forces you into this gamble. As elderly retirees leave the system, an increasing number of new workers are needed to provide new cash injections.

Until 2020 and the government induced recession, Australia has had continuous growth since 1991. The politicians are addicted to this success, stability and tax base. At some stage, Australia will be less attractive to intelligent, productive workers as with over-population, the quality of life will decrease, medical services will decrease and the infrastructure will decay. The government will resort to less skilled mass-immigration hoping to prop up the scam as it will begin to collapse.

The immigration Ponzi to feed national debt (and pension schemes, medical services) is like a water reservoir. More water going in is needed than coming out, as evaporative losses are evaporated as management fees.

It took Australia's government 15 years after introducing Superannuation to list reliable investors that won't siphon your pension on management fees and gambling losses. As with any fresh source of currency, investment operators popped-up to play with the public's futures when Superannuation was introduced with no regulation.

Mass-Immigration and Multiculturalism

Mass-immigration adds more tax units to the population of the country. It also means the same initial Wealth passes more hands and therefore experiences more taxation removals (velocity of currency). Overall the immigrant population facilitate the transmittal of the Corporate Wealth to the government via more taxations.

If these persons are from varying backgrounds their local skill set is negligible. They may not know the local electricity voltage or building codes, therefore they must sub-contract more labour to others, increasing velocity (tax pyramid).

Mass-immigration of the illiterate, unskilled and polygamous large families creates a greater burden on government provided services and welfare. This in turn puts a greater burden on the wealth producers to provide the tax base to pay for it all.

Increasingly, in European welfare states, the single male population is providing for the single female population and for the mass-immigrant population.

The mass-immigrant population is less likely to contribute willingly towards the country that accepted them, as they have no historical stake in the country and they haven't created a similar system in their own; thereby mistrusting it to continue. If it ceased to exist, they would simply move to the next country providing welfare and services rather than patriotically build-up the country that accepted them.

Usury as Pyramid

Trickle Down Economics of the Reagan era proposes that the wealthy cannot help but divest some of their cash which trickles down through society. Industrialists can't do all the work themselves, employees are needed and they spend themselves such as large powerboats status symbols. Industrialists fund investment. This implies an inherent hierarchical system with a 3 tiered class system: Wealth Class, Manager Class and Worker Class.

Increasingly, the wealthy are not industrialists but moneylenders and bankers. No real wealth is being created; the money supply (liquidity) is simple being re-distributed back up the food chain towards those at the top, the 1%. Investing needs less hands compared to industry, so the wealthy employ less. The Trickle Down Effect starts to dry up and the tax base is reduced as less population is being taxed where the wealth lies, pushing a greater burden on those who are in the Manager and Worker Class.

The usury fake debt currency printing system by central banks ensures there will always be debt. Even if you do nothing, the fact that you have some currency notes in your pocket, their very existence, means a national debt exists and is increasing because of interest. If you do nothing, the debt increases and your future ability to pay this debt deceases. If you stand still, you face poverty.

Endless Wars

Wars provide access to new resources for central banks and raise the national debt. One easily researched war is the Boer War in South Africa. A more recent example is the war against Libya's leader Gadaffi who tried opt out of the Cabal's currency printing system. War to reduce population was forwarded by The Report from Iron Mountain.

"Although all the nations of Europe have tried and trodden every path of force and folly in a fruitless quest of the same object, yet we still expect to find in juggling tricks and banking dreams, that money can be made out of nothing, and in sufficient quantity to meet the expenses of a heavy war..."

Thomas Jefferson, (Letter to James Monroe, January 1, 1815).

Britain and the USA are in a permanent state of war, yet their populations are decreasing in wealth. As the booty from wars go to the globalist bankers, the tax burden for warring is placed onto the population.

The End Result of Central Banking is Poverty

Commonly Leftist Useful Idiots exclaim that Capitalism is the cause of misery on the planet. That notion is a mentally inserted falsehood. Capitalism is the mutual exchange of goods. If Japan wants energy,

Capitalism provides and in return, if Americans want Japanese cars, Capitalism again provides. Every time you go to the supermarket, you enforce the good need of Capitalism. Shopping feels good because it is Natural.

Capitalism is the natural exchange mechanism that benefits both parties – otherwise they wouldn't partake in it. It is in great contrast to the Central Bank exchange mechanism, where all parties lose except those with power to print more medium of exchange (currency).

Capitalism has existed since mankind lived a Hunter & Gatherer existence. A stone axe could be bartered for a spear. The products needed to create the stone axe and spear could have been sourced by Capitalistic exchange amongst Gatherers and Artisans.

The notion of a medium of exchange, a currency, outwardly appears to make barter of goods fairer, as both persons agree on the value of the currency. The value of the currency may be agreed upon by the Capitalists involved in the exchange but behind the scenes, really that is the provenance of the Central Bankers. They are simply paper notes with numbers that the public have unsubstantiated psychological confidence in that actually represent the nation's debt.

The Capitalistic barter of Goods is parasitised by two entities: Central Banks & Government. The very use of the printed currency means the Central Bank is getting a cut (through the bonds to printed currency and debt shenanigans) and governments charge a plethora of taxes other than the direct GST/VAT/Tariffs on the actual goods being exchanged. Those taxes are redistributed upwards to the bank to service (not repay) the national debt. The parasitism depicted:

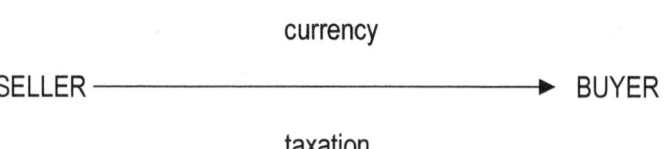

Therefore, the presence of a Central Bank in your country means you are slowly heading in a cancerous, terminal decline towards poverty.

"If the American people ever allow private banks (Federal Reserve) to control the issue of their currency, they will deprive the people of all property until their children wake-up homeless on the continent their father built."

Thomas Jefferson, 1809

The number of homeless people living on the streets in the West has sky-rocketed since the opulent 1960s. If you had $10,000 in the bank in that period, you were wealthy. If you had kept that in a deposit account, today it would barely get you through one year's living expenses. The public is deliberately being impoverished and enslaved. It particularly erodes the middle class creating a banker 1% and everyone else.

As the Great Reset of the World Economic Forum advertises, "You will own nothing". Presumably, the 1% of bankers will own everything from your home, to your food production, to your TV, the water you drink and even the air you breathe!

Fear Propaganda

The Report from Iron Mountain suggested Alien Invasion, Environmental Disaster and Endless War to instill fear, gain additional control and deplete populations.

Agenda 2021, Agenda 2030, the Great Replacement and the Great Reset are top down implementations or revolutions from the globalists that use central banking to destroy the wealth we created and the wealth that gives us independence.

Several other planned revolutions are out there. The Rockefeller Operation Lockstep describes how governments can take further control of their paralysed populations and render them more submissive through use of a pandemic.

Communism by COVID (SARS-2)

Prior to the COVID Pandemic of 2020, Central Banks had been increasing their holdings of gold for 2-3 years. This could only mean a currency printing orgy had been planned as gold is the fractional reserve real money used for currency printing.

Immediately, upon government imposed Lockdowns, the world's Central Banks started printing and the politicians started throwing the newly counterfeited cash around like confetti at a wedding. In addition, government advertising concerning mental illnesses such as depression hit the airwaves.

Government cash handouts included increased and additional welfare payments to unsolicited cash injections into small businesses. Certain areas of the economy such as mining, energy, construction and transport (except airline) were considered essential. However, overwhelmingly, small businesses where the public congregated such as cafes, restaurants and bars were shut down. After a few months this became a government induced recession forced on the public using Coercive Control Measures. The economy was kept going by welfare handouts from the Central Bank currency printing & debt faking machine which slowed the induced depression.

In Australia, the Treasurer, Tax Office and central bank operated in cohesion to print currency, throw it around and rack up an enormous national debt from nowhere.

This is a soft route to Communism, a One World Government, using the COVID pandemic as cover. An obedient population, huge unrepayable debt, debt slavery, a worthless currency and employment by government.

"The powers of financial capitalism had a far-reaching plan, nothing less than to create a world system of financial control in private hands able to dominate the political system of each country and the economy of the world as a whole… Their secret is that they have annexed from governments, monarchies, and republics the power to create the world's money…"

Professor Carroll Quigley

Tragedy & Hope

PART E - FINALE

This short book has demonstrated by theory and examples that Central Banks are an exchange mechanism through which your life's work is stolen.

Whether you toil the land, sweat in construction, build cars, create, invent, planned the moon landings or a mission to Mars; be it manual or cerebral, your existence and very life force is stolen. It is stolen in the payment you receive which is in a currency printed by the local Central Bank. They determine the value of your work through manipulating the amount of currency they print as FIAT. Your work is exchanged for worthless currency and converted into real wealth (gold) which the Central bank keeps for itself.

If extra currency is pumped into the economy, money is easily available and loans are cheap. This induces many to adopt large loans. The interest rates are then deliberately increased to squeeze more sweat from the debtor. This can reach a stage where they become slaves on their own livelihood and can even lose their life's work overnight from a foreclosure.

Manipulating interest rates by pumping more currency into an economy causes inflated asset bubbles (property, Stock Market). When the currency elasticity is tightened, interest rates rise, those in debt try to dump assets (real estate, stock market) and those in the know (through their friends at Central banks) gobble-up the bargains from the misery of the small guy's fear.

Pensions are often heavily contributed into the Stock Market. The Stock Market may always go up over time but the currency used to liquidate assets from sold shares, always goes down. Currency printing is sometimes described as an unseen stealth tax.

Every single effort you do in life is taxed. That tax is not used on schools, hospitals and roads (or the world would be covered in them), it is used to service but not re-pay, a debt faked out of this air by printing of FIAT currency.

Your life's work is paid in that FIAT currency which has no inherent value and can be either reduced in purchasing power by printing more (causing inflation and lower interest rates) or by being literally burned (causing deflation and higher interest rates), although over time the currency is only ever depreciated (devalued).

Governments work for Central Banks by taxing you to service (not re-pay) a debt faked out of thin air. Central banks loot the wealth from a country and all wealth creation is re-distributed back upward through a pyramid to that Central Bank.

It is the crime of the millennium.

The Central Banks decide the medium of payment for your toil; FIAT currency. Therefore, they exchange your work for worthless currency. Then they convert your toil for real assets such as gold they keep themselves. This is slavery on a global scale.

In Talmudic prophesy, all the world's property and gold will reside with the Talmudists while the world's population are their slaves. The Talmud identifies real wealth as property and gold, as in feudal days before central banking was given the power to use fractional reserves for currency printing.

Real wealth is land, property, gold and silver. Silver has been used as money for exchange in goods and services transactions for millennia e.g. Judas sold out Jesus who took on the bankers and received 30 silver coins.

BIBLIOGRAPHY

The following literature was used in creating this book:

Sarah Emery – Imperialism in America, 1893

Mary Hobart – The Secret of the Rothschilds, 1898

Arthur Cherap-Spiridovich – The Hidden Hand, 1926

Charles Lindbergh – Banking and Currency and the Money Trust, 1913

Louis McFadden – Speech on the Federal Reserve, 10.06.1932

George F Dillon – Grand Orient Freemasonry Unmasked as the secret power behind communism, 1965

Anthony Sutton – Wall Street and the Bolshevik Revolution, 1973

Anthony Sutton – The Federal Reserve Conspiracy, 1974

Eustace Mullins – Secrets of the Federal Reserve, 1974

Murray Rothbard – The Mystery of Banking, 1983

G Edward Griffin – The Creature from Jekyll Island, 1994

Chris Leithner - The Evil Princes of Martin Place, 2011

Michael Hoffman – Usury in Christendom, 2013

Stephen Mitford Goodson – A History of Central Banking and the Enslavement of Mankind, 2014

Michael Hudson – Killing the Host: how financial parasites and debt bondage destroy the global economy, 2015

Seamus bin Shylockeen – The Age of Confusion, 2018

Useful Video and websites:

The American Dream Film

The History of Money – Gold Silver Mike Maloney

ACKNOWLEDGEMENTS

The preliminary text was sent to several for review. A special thanks is reserved for Chris Ghysel for his time and thoroughness.